THE ART OF THE

PRE~RAPHAELITES

Edmund Swinglehurst

A Compilation of Works from the

BRIDGEMAN ART LIBRARY

SHOOTING STAR PRESS

Shooting Star Press Inc
230 Fifth Avenue, New York, New York 10001

Pre-Raphaelites

© Parragon Book Service Ltd 1994

This edition printed for:
Shooting Star Press, Inc.
230 Fifth Avenue - Suite 1212
New York, NY 10001

ISBN   1 56924 180 5

Printed in Italy

Editor: Alexa Stace
Designer: Robert Mathias

The publishers would like to thank Joanna Hartley
at the Bridgeman Art Library for her invaluable help

The Pre-Raphaelites

THE PRE-RAPHAELITE BROTHERHOOD, identified in its earliest work by the mysterious initials, PRB, was an association of painters, formed in London in 1848. Its chief members were William Holman Hunt, John Everett Millais and Dante Gabriel Rossetti, the oldest of whom, Hunt, was still only 21. As a group, the Brotherhood lasted for little more than a decade, but the impetus it gave to leading Victorian art in a new direction lasted until the early years of the 20th century.

Until the Brotherhood made its mark, British art was very much dominated by the Royal Academy, founded in the early years of George III's reign, and its first President, Joshua Reynolds. Despite the work of men such as Turner and Constable, the style of painting favoured by the Royal Academy tended towards that of the Old Masters, with copious use of brown paint. The three youthful Pre-Raphaelites deliberately challenged the established view of art, drawing up a manifesto of their intentions and publishing them in the four issues of a periodical called *The Germ*. They would paint direct from nature, with objective truthfulness and genuine ideas in sympathy with what was direct and heartfelt in the art of the past – particularly art before Raphael.

To emulate the work of the great Italian artists who had preceded Raphael, the painters of the Brotherhood made meticulous studies of the colours in nature, reproducing them brightly and clearly and working them into a wet, white ground. They went to inordinate lengths to find exact models for the settings and people in their pictures. In their desire to depict genuine, deeply significant themes they turned to the Bible for inspiration. Among the most significant of their early paintings were Hunt's *Light of the World* and *The Hireling Shepherd,* Millais' *Christ in the House of his Parents* and Rossetti's two versions of the Annunciation theme.

Initially, critics, including Charles Dickens, were hostile. They disliked the kind of realism that showed Christ's father as a working man with dirty fingernails and the Virgin as an ordinary young girl. The PRB was seen to be setting itself up as something better than Raphael; its members were also suspected of Romanist tendencies (this was the period of the Oxford Movement). But the great critic John Ruskin defended them strongly and the new painters soon had their admirers, particularly among the increasingly affluent middle classes of the Midlands and North of England.

The high-minded aims of the Brotherhood proved insufficient to hold the interest of Rossetti's fertile imagination and the restless skills of Millais for long. Only Hunt stayed faithful to the ideals of the Brotherhood. The other two developed in other directions, replacing biblical inspiration with that of the medieval world, the plays of Shakespeare and other sources made popular by the Romantic movement of the early 19th century.

Though the Brotherhood dissolved in about 1853, the new climate in art was one with which many other artists identified.

Foremost among them was Ford Madox Brown, a friend of the Brotherhood artists who shared their ideas. Brown, who had been born abroad and received his artistic training in Europe, was not much drawn to the biblical aspects of the Brotherhood's work and its close identification with the religious ethos of the time in England. His early paintings were more Romantic in character, often based on the poetry of Byron.

As Queen Victoria's reign lengthened, the British became more aware of their Imperial role. Interest grew in classical literature and the history of ancient Greece and Rome, as well as in the legendary medieval past of Britain itself. In art, Edward Burne-Jones was the prolific master of both the classical and the medieval scene, producing works like the *Pygmalion* series and *King Cophetua and the Beggarmaid* in which the theme of the moral superiority of nobility of character above worldly wealth began to appear.

The classical theme, once established, provided a splendid opportunity for artists to combine sex and art in a tasteful manner acceptable to Victorian sensibility. Encouraged by the Royal Academy, artists produced more and more delectable paintings of Greek and Roman ladies at their bath and in other intimate situations. The technical standards of these paintings, set by the Pre-Raphaelites, were very high and were maintained throughout the period, for Victorian patrons would not accept anything other than expert craftsmanship.

Among the new generation of classical painters were men like Leighton (given a peerage), Poynter and Alma-Tadema (both knighted), whose idealized visions of the lives of ancient Greeks and Romans had the comfortable serenity of fairy tales.

There were other currents at work in the stream of art, an important one having been set in motion by Rossetti, who was a poet as well as a painter. He developed an idiosyncratic style full of mysterious undertones, using colour not to describe nature realistically but to suggest mood and feeling. This became the artistic theme which Walter Pater, an admirer of the Pre-Raphaelites, expressed in his writings on art, which were to stir up new ideas and attitudes. These ideas, though not to everyone's taste, represented a change in attitude prevalent in the more affluent society of the century's close, who saw in the cultured hedonism of such paintings as Godward's *Dolce Far Niente* or Solomon's *The Lovers* an acceptable philosophy of life.

Alongside this intimate boudoir art ran a continuing tendency to paint epic scenes. John Byam Shaw's *Love the Conqueror,* branded by one critic as trivial, was painted in 1899, when Impressionism, which had seized the high ground of art in France and was opening the gates to 20th-century painting, was already a generation old. In truth, Pre-Raphaelitism had had its day; although it hung on in British art until after World War I, it no longer represented the feelings and ideas of society.

△ **The Hireling Shepherd** 1851   William Holman Hunt (1827-1910)

Oil on canvas

WILLIAM HOLMAN HUNT was one of the founder members of the Pre-Raphaelite Brotherhood, with Dante Gabriel Rossetti and John Everett Millais. This painting was one of the first to incorporate the aims of the Brotherhood, which were to paint realistic and truthful paintings with a high moral tone. In search of a suitable background for *The Hireling Shepherd* Hunt went with his friend Millais to Ewell in Surrey. Having found what he wanted, he painted a detailed landscape in which he left a blank space for the figures, which he painted in later. The painting is full of the symbolism characteristic of Hunt's work. The shepherd, clearly a hireling, is evidently neglecting the sheep and is thus, by implication, not a 'good' shepherd. The small barrel of beer at his waist suggests a taste for pleasure above duty. The shepherdess, who is feeding green apples to a lamb, is also evidently careless of her responsibilities. This high-minded approach to art, perfectly in tune with public taste at the time, ensured the painting a good reception when it was exhibited at the Royal Academy.

▷ The Light of the World
1853   William Holman Hunt

Oil on canvas on panel

HUNT WROTE TO HIS FRIEND
William Bell Scott to explain
that in undertaking this
subject he had felt impelled to
do so by divine command. His
original intention had been to
make it a daytime scene, but
he changed his mind at the
idea of the challenge of a night
picture, something he had
never attempted before. As
was his usual habit, Hunt set
off with a friend, C.A. Collins,
in search of a background.
After walking with a lantern in
the neighbourhood of Ewell
station he found a workman's
hut which he decided to use.
He also found an orchard
where he erected a straw hut
from which he could study the
effect of moonlight through
the trees. For the face of Christ
he created a composite of the
faces of friends and 'departed
heroes'. When first exhibited,
the painting did not receive
the acclaim that Hunt had
hoped for. In the course of
time, largely through the
publication of engravings, it
became one of the most potent
icons of the 19th and early
20th centuries.

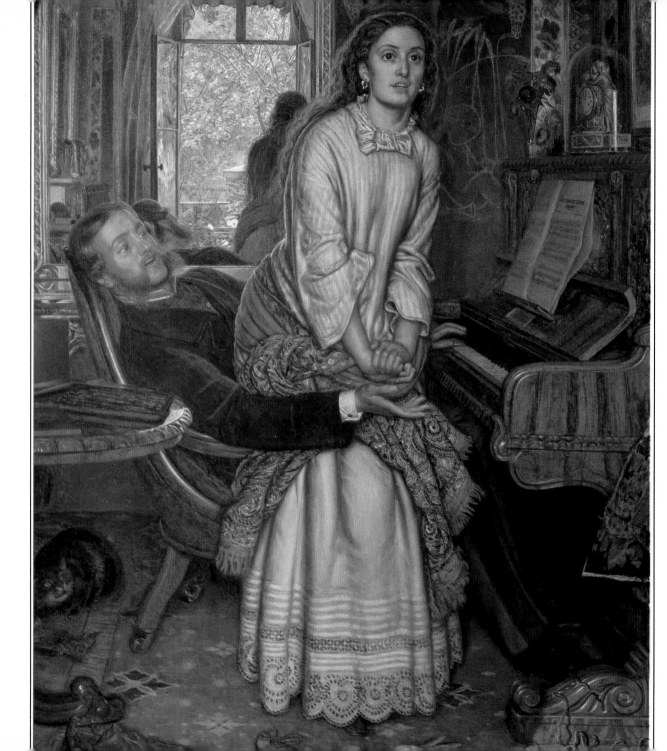

◁ **The Awakening Conscience**
1853   William Holman Hunt

Oil on canvas

THIS PAINTING is a perfect example of Hunt's preoccupation with finding exactly the right setting for his narrative. Although the exact location of the room in this painting has not been identified, there is no doubt that Hunt found a real room that suited his purpose and then filled it with the symbolic matter that would point the moral of his painting. The expression in the young woman's eyes as she draws away from the man tells the story well enough, but to make sure that everyone understands, Hunt has laid a soiled glove on the carpet at her feet and introduced a cat from which a bird is trying to escape. On the piano is a piece of music entitled 'Oft in the stilly night' and above it a corner of a painting, *The Woman Taken in Adultery*. The young man at the piano

Detail

appears oblivious to the young woman's awakening; so, according to Ruskin, were the public when the picture was first shown. The critic of the art magazine, *The Athenaeum,* opined that many thought the painting represented a quarrel between brother and sister.

▷ **The Scapegoat** 1854-5
William Holman Hunt

Oil on canvas

VISITING THE HOLY LAND in 1854 in search of scenes to use in paintings of the life of Christ, Hunt hit on the idea for *The Scapegoat,* from the account in Leviticus of how, as part of the Jewish ritual of Atonement, two goats are selected, one to be sacrificed and the other to be released into the wilderness to atone for the sins of the community. The goat became, in Hunt's concept of the ritual, Jesus Christ himself, 'Despised and rejected of men . . .
. . . wounded for our transgressions'. Hunt found a goat, tethered it near the Dead Sea and studied and painted it for days on end. He made two versions of *The Scapegoat,* the first including a rainbow that appeared as he painted and the second, without the rainbow, of a goat with a white fleece, symbol of purity and lack of sin. In both versions he included the skull of an ibex, though in this version the skull and horns have become separated. The ibex skull was added to oblige a friend who had told Hunt that he should have used a goat with curved horns.

◁ **The Lantern Maker's Courtship: a Street Scene in Cairo** 1854
William Holman Hunt

Oil on canvas

HUNT VISITED CAIRO in 1854, before the opening of the Suez Canal made Egypt a tourist destination. He was much impressed by the, to him, alien culture and by the street life, which gave him the idea for this genre painting. Making a drawing of the shop where he had witnessed this scene, Hunt found himself up against the Islamic prohibition of the depiction of people. He finally found a young man prepared to pose but had to paint the girl from memory. In the background he included his friend Millais, arguing with shopkeepers, and a camel blocking the street. Owing to these and other difficulties, Hunt did not finish the painting in time to exhibit it at that year's Royal Academy show, though it was much admired by those he showed it to privately. Hunt later made another version of it.

▷ **The Lady of Shalott** 1886-1905 William Holman Hunt

Oil on canvas

HUNT FIRST BEGAN to work out ideas for a painting based on Tennyson's poem 'The Lady of Shalott' in 1850, but did not begin painting it until 1886. By this time the status of women in society had begun to change and the movement for women's emancipation was beginning to make itself heard. Perhaps it was this that made Hunt choose to paint the moment when the Lady of Shalott, condemned to see life only as a reflection in a mirror, decides to rebel and looks out of the window at Sir Lancelot. Her punishment for this will be death, though there is no hint of this in Hunt's painting, which he did not finish to exhibition standard until nearly 20 years after he started it. It has been called the last great Pre-Raphaelite painting and is indeed one of Hunt's finest works, its swirling lines making it a precursor of art nouveau.

◁ **Christ in the House of His Parents** 1850 John Everett Millais (1826-96)

Oil on canvas

THIS WAS MILLAIS'S first religious painting and was exhibited at the Royal Academy in 1850, where its realism caused a furore. The conservatism of academic paintings of the day, with their dark brown bitumen and idealized subjects, was what the Pre-Raphaelites had set out to defy, so the reaction to this picture could be seen as a good start for the Brotherhood. The public and art critics objected to the painting because it showed Christ's family as ordinary people, to the extent of depicting Joseph with dirty fingernails. Even Charles Dickens, tolerant about other matters, described the Christ child as 'a hideous, wry-necked, blubbering, red-haired boy in a night-gown'. The publicity excited by the painting provoked Queen Victoria into requesting a private viewing. Her opinion is not known, but Millais is quoted as saying that he hoped the painting 'would not have a bad effect on her mind'.

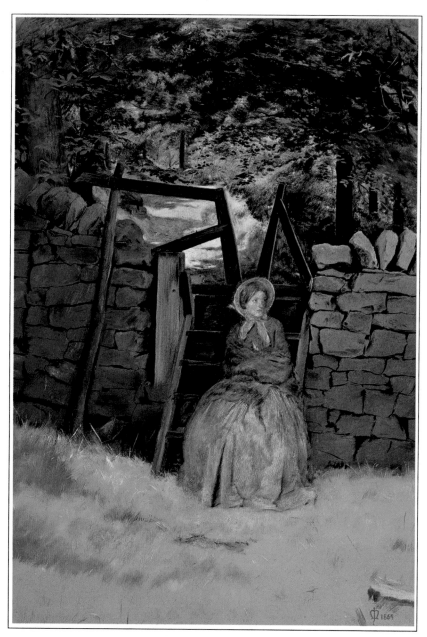

◁ **Waiting** 1854
John Everett Millais

Oil on panel

THIS SMALL PICTURE painted on a panel was probably done in springtime, to judge by the vegetation. It has a freshness of colour about it which is one of the distinguishing features of Millais' early work. It seems to have been a study for a later painting entitled *A Highland Lassie,* for which the model was Euphemia Chalmers Gray whom Millais married in 1855. It has also been suggested that the model for the waiting woman was Holman Hunt's girlfriend but there is no proof of this other than that Hunt and Millais were close friends. The painting has the air of a moment in time seized and recorded, much as the Impressionists were to do later in the century.

▷ **Autumn Leaves** 1855-56
John Everett Millais

Oil on canvas

WRITING TO AN AMERICAN reviewer of this painting, Millais agreed that it was not intended to be a narrative picture but one of mood. 'I intended the picture to awaken by its solemnity the deepest religious reflection', he wrote. The setting is the garden of the Millais home, Annat Lodge, in Perth, Scotland, and the girls burning leaves are Alice, sister of Millais's wife, Effie, (in the centre) and friends. Effie described the painting of the picture and the patience of the models in some detail and reported Millais's words, 'He never had such good models. When they were not wanted they sat in the kitchen, helped to peel potatoes or watched the door or sat still looking into the fire for hours in perfect idleness, quite happy.' Millais sold the painting to James Eden, a collector who owned a bleaching works , for £700; Eden later exchanged it with another collector.

Detail

▷ **Trust Me**   John Everett Millais

Oil on canvas

THE PRE-RAPHAELITES' concern for moral values and social behaviour derived from the new society that was being created in Britain as a result of the Industrial Revolution, along with the first questionings of old-established values. The resulting conflict was a subject that interested the Pre-Raphaelite painters. In this picture, Millais records what was perhaps a not unfamiliar situation in a middle-class household such as his own: a father demands to see the letter that has arrived in the postbag he is holding and his daughter is reluctant to show what she considers to be her private correspondence.

▷ **Ophelia** 1852   John Everett Millais

Oil on canvas

Ophelia was painted at about the same time as Holman Hunt's *Hireling Shepherd*. Millais found the stream that provided the setting for his painting near Ewell, where Hunt had also found settings for his pictures. Millais' painting is full of Shakespearean allusions: the rose in the dead Ophelia's hand is a reference to her brother Laertes's description of her as 'the Rose of May' and the robin in the undergrowth is a reminder of Ophelia's song 'For bonny sweet robin is all my joy'. A true Pre-Raphaelite, Millais spent a great deal of time on the exact reproduction of the stream and the overhanging trees. Despite his care, after it was exhibited (it was hung next to Hunt's *Hireling Shepherd*) the painting's colour deteriorated and Millais was obliged to retouch it. The model was Elizabeth Siddal, later Rossetti's wife. Millais made her pose fully dressed in a bathtub, as a result of which she, not surprisingly, caught cold.

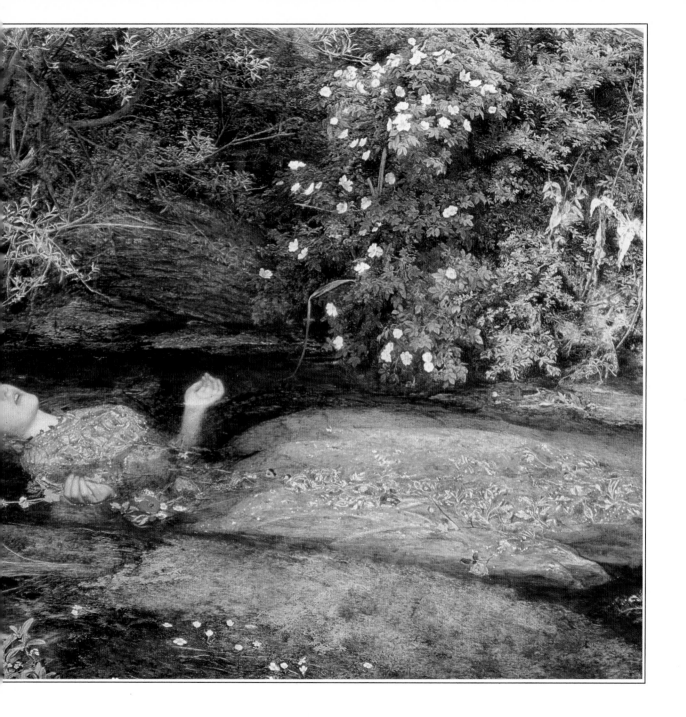

▷ **Sir Isumbras at the Ford: A Dream of the Past** 1857
John Everett Millais

Oil on canvas

THE KINDLY OLD KNIGHT and trusting children represent a Victorian view of the relationship between the old and young and was no doubt painted, like much of Millais's later work, with an eye on public sentiment. The legendary Sir Isumbras was a haughty lord who became more tolerant and soft-hearted after a series of misfortunes came his way. Millais evidently had high hopes for this work; when it did not find a buyer at the Royal Academy Exhibition of 1857, where it was criticized by Ruskin, he took it back to his studio and kicked a hole in it. In fact, Millais was not really happy with his treatment of the horse, which had come out larger than he intended. The size of the horse so worried Millais that he asked his friend, Tom Taylor, a journalist,to write a stanza justifying the horse's size.

◁ **The Boyhood of Raleigh** 1870 John Everett Millais

Oil on canvas

CHEAPLY AVAILABLE PRINTS of this painting hung in nearly every schoolroom in Britain for decades, its inspirational character reminding everyone of Britain's hard-won role as the mistress of the world's oceans. By the time Millais painted this work, he was well settled in his marriage to Effie, former wife of John Ruskin, and he himself was a well-regarded member of the artistic establishment, having been elected RA in 1863. From this period, his style became looser and his subjects more popular in character. Less uncompromising than Hunt, Millais became more sentimental as he grew older and completed his life's work with such paintings as *Cherry Ripe* and *Bubbles* which, though immensely popular among the public, did little to enhance his artistic reputation.

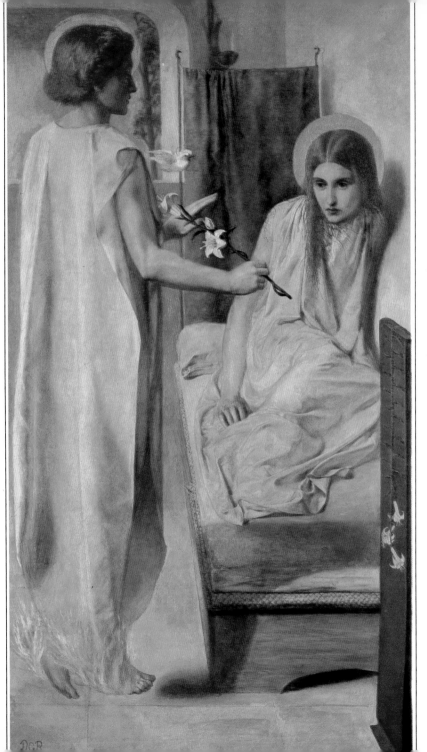

◁ **The Annunciation:
Ecce Ancilla Domini** 1850
Dante Gabriel Rossetti
(1828-82)

Oil on canvas

ROSSETTI EXHIBITED this
painting at the Royal Academy
in 1850, when Hunt showed
his *Early Britons Sheltering a
Missionary from the Druids* and
Millais his *Christ in the House of
His Parents* (page 17). All three
treated Christian subjects in
accordance with the beliefs of
their Pre-Raphaelite
Brotherhood, formed just two
years previously. In painting
this Annunciation in such a
realistic manner Rossetti was
breaking with tradition. Italian
Renaissance artists showed the
Virgin as a holy figure, isolated
from everyday life by her
situation. Rossetti's Virgin is an
ordinary girl, bewildered and
frightened by the news that
the angel has just given her.
This unorthodox approach,
which enraged large sections
of the art-loving public, was in
keeping with the Pre-
Raphaelite commitment to
paint truthfully.

▷ **The Annunciation** 1855
Dante Gabriel Rossetti

Watercolour

THIS IS A VERY different
Annunciation from the one
subtitled *Ecce Ancilla Domini*
(page 28). The figure of the
Virgin was based on a drawing
of Elizabeth Siddal which
Rossetti had done in 1854.
Siddal had been discovered by
Deverell, a friend of the Pre-
Raphaelites, working as a sales
girl and he introduced her to
the group who used her as a
model. From about 1852 she
modelled only for Rossetti and
the two were married in 1860.
Two years later, she was found
dying from an overdose of
laudanum, taken in a
depressed state after the death
of her newborn daughter. In
this Annunciation Rossetti has
adopted a freer brushwork
than in the earlier one, though
he is still using a Pre-
Raphaelite symbolism: the
Virgin is raising a cupped
hand of water, symbol of
purity, as the dove hovers over
her. The watercolour was one
of a series of scenes from the
life of the Virgin which
Rossetti worked on
throughout the 1850s.

◁ **The Beloved (The Bride)**
1865-6
Dante Gabriel Rossetti

Oil on canvas

IN ROSSETTI'S WORK the religious idealism of the early Pre-Raphaelite Brotherhood gradually gave way to a new kind of spirituality in which sensuality was a heady ingredient. In this painting the biblical reference is to the Song of Solomon: 'My beloved is mine and I am his. Let him kiss me with the kisses of his mouth: for thy love is better than wine'. The Victorian inclination to conceal real motives for their actions led F. G. Stephens to describe this painting as an expression of 'the power of women to move men'. The model for the young woman, showing herself to her betrothed surrounded by her friends and a young black girl, was a girl called Maria Ford.

May Morris 1872
Dante Gabriel Rossetti

Coloured chalks

▷ *Overleaf, page 32*

MAY MORRIS was one of the two daughters of the poet and craftsman, William Morris and his wife Jane. In this beautiful study, Rossetti has given May a strong look of her mother, with whom Rossetti was infatuated, although there was no question of intimacy between them. Almost every woman he painted had something of Jane about her. This painting bears the inscription 'M.M. aetat X1872', the year of Rossetti's schizophrenic collapse. Both May and her sister Jenny were fond of Rossetti, who often asked after them. On one such occasion Jane replied, rather strangely, that May was a delicate child and would not drag through a long life. 'So much the better for her'. In fact, May lived well into the 20th century, quite long enough to edit her father's works and to write a biography of him.

◁ **The Lady of Pity** c 1875
Dante Gabriel Rossetti

Oil on canvas

The Lady of Pity is a typically romantic view of Jane Morris as Rossetti saw her, with her grey eyes, full lips and abundant hair all emphasized. Rossetti found the combination of sensuality and intellectuality in Jane tantalizing and he had a close but not physical relationship with the wife of his friend William Morris. In the scroll under the portrait Rossetti, who was of Italian origin, has written 'color d'amore e di pietà sembiante' (the colour of love and appearance of pity). Rossetti's Italian Romanticism aroused some criticism. A reviewer in the *Contemporary Review* in 1871 referred to Rossetti's poetry as 'The fleshly school of poetry, never spiritual, never tender, always self-conscious and aesthetic . . . a stupendous preponderance of sensibility and sickly animalism'. This greatly upset Rossetti ,who soon after suffered a schizophrenic breakdown.

▷ **Astarte Syriaca** 1877
Dante Gabriel Rossetti

Oil on canvas

ASTARTE, the Syrian goddess of
love, was both caring and
cruel. By using Jane Morris as
the model for her Rossetti was
perhaps saying something
about his inner torments
concerning Jane. Perhaps, too,
he was saying something about
the theme of unrequited love,
which had a great vogue in
Victorian times. Other heroes
and heroines admired for their
abnegation included Dante
and Beatrice and Petrarch and
Laura, who also featured in
the Victorian iconography of
love. During the hours she
spent posing for this painting
Jane discovered how much
Rossetti was addicted to the
drug chloral and this, as well
as her awareness of his
obsession with her, may have
decided her to distance herself
a little from the artist.

◁ **The Day-dream** 1880
Dante Gabriel Rossetti

Oil on canvas

ROSSETTI PAINTED this splendid
work after Jane Morris had
ceased to pose regularly for
him; it was done from an
earlier drawing of Jane sitting
in a tree at Kelmscott, the
home that Rossetti shared with
the Morrises on the Thames.
The book she is holding is a
reference to her love of
reading and the sycamore tree
with its unfolding buds is a
symbol of spring. The spray of
honeysuckle in Jane's hand is
also a symbol, its heady scent
and tongue-like petals
suggesting the sexual love that
Rosetti felt for her but which
could never be satisfied. When
this picture was painted
Rossetti had abandoned the
Pre-Raphaelite principles of
his early years and his
aesthetic art style was well
developed.

▷ **Manfred on the Jungfrau**
1842
Ford Madox Brown (1821-93)

Oil on canvas

FORD MADDOX BROWN's birth in France and 10 years of study as an artist in Bruges and Antwerp predisposed him to Romantic subjects in the style of Delacroix, though his admiration for the Romantics was tempered by his admiration for the draughtsmanship of David, the classical painter of Napoleonic France. This early painting, based on a poem by that most romantic of English poets, Lord Byron, shows the two tendencies combining in Brown's work. He has chosen to depict the moment in Byron's poem, 'Manfred', when the hero is about to leap off the mountain to his death. The expression on the face is frozen in a dramatic grimace and the body language is derived from French rhetorical paintings. The painting was actually completed in Paris about 1842, a year after he had conceived the composition in Brussels.

▷ **Stages of Cruelty** 1856-90   Ford Madox Brown

Oil on canvas

ALTHOUGH FORD MADOX BROWN was never a member of the Pre-Raphaelite Brotherhood, he felt great sympathy for their aims and ideas. Before returning to England in the late 1840s, he had picked up ideas similar to the Pre-Raphaelites from the Nazarenes, a German-based group of painters who admired mediaeval themes and style and painted in bright clear colours. Brown met Rossetti after his Continental studies and was so impressed by his work that he asked to receive lessons from him. Brown shared the Pre-Raphaelite taste for everyday subjects with moral implications and symbolic meanings. In this painting he uses the lovers for his narrative and makes his symbolic points with the convolvulus, signifying entanglements, climbing up the steps. The small girl about to hit the dog reflects the often unthinking nature of cruelty. Brown had some difficulty in completing the painting because the models for the lovers were unreliable and also because no one showed any interest in commissioning it. He eventually sold it in 1887.

△ **Work** 1852-65   Ford Madox Brown

Oil on canvas

IN *Work*, painted partly in the open air in Heath Street, Hampstead, he shows the various categories of work, from manual labour to intellectual work (symbolized by Carlyle and F. D. Maurice on the right of the picture). Brown had spent two years as a teacher in Maurice's Working Men's College. The painting was made on a white ground, rather than the brown currently used, in order to enhance the colour. The painting was almost completed when a potential buyer, a Mr Plint, insisted that it lacked moral and religious significance and obliged Brown to add a lady distributing tracts (on the left). Unfortunately, Plint died before Brown finished his work, but when it was exhibited in 1865 Plint's estate bought it.

▷ **The Last Of England**
1852-55   Ford Madox Brown

Oil on panel

THE POIGNANCY of this picture of unhappy emigrants must have struck a chord in many hearts at a time when many Britons were being forced to emigrate in search of a better life. Perhaps Brown's own situation as a struggling and impecunious artist contributed to his depiction of the sad desperation of the couple in this famous painting. He himself had reached the point of considering whether to emigrate to India but was saved by the sale of this painting. The ship on which the couple and their child are leaving is evidently on a long voyage, for fresh vegetables have been tied along the rails and in the background is a lifeboat also full of provisions · a cabin boy is selecting some for the first meal aboard.

1892-93   George Frederick
Watts (1817-1904)

Oil on canvas

WATTS WAS A TALENTED young
man who first exhibited at the
Royal Academy at the age of
20 and later won a prize in a
competition for the decoration
of the Houses of Parliament.
The money enabled him to go
to Italy where he studied the
Renaissance painters. On his
return to England he became a
successful portraitist and a
painter of allegorical scenes
which the public associated
with the highest form of art.
She Shall Be Called Woman is a
typical Watts female nude with
a high-sounding title. His
technique was very individual
for he did not like the glossy
finish of most contemporary
oil paintings and would put his
colours on blotting paper to
diminish their oil content. He
also had a freer style than such
contemporaries as Leighton
and Alma-Tadema. Watts'
declared aims were to paint
pictures that appealed 'to the
intellect and refined emotions
rather than the senses.'

▷ **Hope** 1885 George Frederick Watts

Oil on canvas

IN THIS PAINTING of a blindfolded woman with a broken lyre Watts was expressing the sentiments of such popular aphorisms as 'Never despair' or 'Where there is life there is hope', though his painting seems to be suggesting the opposite. The Victorian public understood his message, however, and the painting became enormously popular, especially after it was reproduced as an engraving. Watts's talents extended into other branches of the arts; he was a fresco painter and sculptor (one of his statues, *Physical Energy,* is in Kensington Gardens in London). Offered a baronetcy for his contribution to art, Watts refused, though he later accepted the Order of Merit. The best of his work was undoubtedly his portraiture, including studies of Carlyle and Tennyson, which showed a depth of understanding of his subjects' characters.

▷ **Love and the Maiden**
John Roddam Spencer Stanhope (1829-1908)

Oil on canvas

THE INFLUENCE of Spencer Stanhope's lifelong friend Burne-Jones is clearly visible in this painting, in which the god of love approaches a young woman in a wood by the edge of the sea. The painted flowers are typical of the precise Pre-Raphaelite technique in which every inch of the painting is in focus.

The theme belongs to the aesthetic period of paintings of which Rossetti was a protagonist and which nurtured the seeds of art for art's sake, propounded by Walter Pater, friend of the Pre-Raphaelites, whose concepts were criticized for being an encouragement to cultural hedonism.

◁ **Washing Day** John Roddam Spencer Stanhope

SPENCER STANHOPE came from an affluent middle-class family and was educated at Rugby and Christchurch, Oxford. He began to study art with G. F. Watts in 1850, visiting Italy with him in 1853. He became one of the circle of young artists around the Pre-Raphaelites in the mid-1850s and was particularly friendly with Burne-Jones, who influenced his painting and became a lifelong friend. He first exhibited at the Royal Academy in 1859 and later at the Grosvenor Gallery. Like his artist friends, he had a sympathy for ordinary people and often chose subjects showing them at work, though often in an idealized manner. *Washing Day* in which the women wash the clothes while the men get on with the business of fishing, is typical of Stanhope's work.

▷ **Winding the Skein** 1878
Frederic Leighton (1830-96)

Oil on canvas

LEIGHTON, who became the only British artist to be made a peer, had a privileged upbringing thanks to his father, a Scarborough doctor. He ensured that his son was given a thorough classical education and also learnt French, German and Italian, thus gaining some first-hand experience of European culture. This background, and his sociable manner and good looks, ensured Leighton a comfortable place in British society. After he was 25 Leighton's work became more and more influenced by Hellenistic culture which he considered 'the most perfect balance of transcendent gifts' The setting for *Winding the Skein,* a Roman or Greek house with a terrace looking out to sea, suggests the calm, contemplative life which Leighton ascribed to Greek culture, though its very perfection gives it a bland character which subsequent generations have found soporific.

◁ **Phoenicians Trading** 1895   Frederic Leighton

Fresco

TOWARDS THE LAST quarter of the 19th century the Pre-Raphaelite concern with religious and moral subjects gave way to themes of the revival of classical history. Leighton was one of the most important and prolific exponents of the new interest. From his early youth he had been immersed in the classics and a visit to Rome in 1852 had stimulated him further. His own enthusiasm for the subject coincided with a public interest awakened by the publication of Lord Lytton's *Last Days of Ancient Rome* and by the archaeological discoveries at Pompeii and Herculaneum. This picture of sea traders evokes the early days of Rome when Phoenician traders came to the ports of the young Empire, bringing the products and culture of the East.

◁ **Bath of Psyche** c 1890   Frederic Leighton

Oil on canvas

THE CLASSICAL REVIVAL in Britain coincided with the success of British Imperial trade and the increased middle-class affluence which went with it. The new wealthy classes, seeking a cultural background for their new lives, adopted Rome, the greatest empire of the past, as their model. Literature, architecture and art reflected this and also gave an accepted respectability to straightforward nudity, as in this painting which Leighton has associated with the bath of the goddess of love. The nude woman is standing on the edge of a marble bath and is surrounded with Roman columns – all of which give authenticity to the title of his painting.

◁ **On the Temple Steps**
Edward John Poynter
(1836-1919)

Oil on canvas

POYNTER STUDIED painting in
Paris at Charles Gleyre's
studio, where many of the
young artists who were to
become major Impressionists
had their early training. While
there, Poynter met the
American artist Whistler, but
he was not himself drawn into
the vortex of the new
movements in art in France. In
Britain, the young French
painters were regarded as
amateurs who hardly knew
how to draw. Poynter devoted
himself to correct drawing and
classical themes, and thus
found favour with the British
art-buying public. He became
an R A in 1876 and was
knighted in 1896. In this
painting, Poynter's debt to the
Pre-Raphaelites shows in the
precise drawing and great
attention to detail. In choosing
the subject Poynter has
expressed the hidden love of
the exotic that lurked beneath
many a Victorian waistcoat
and which encouraged much
travel to the Middle East.

◁ **A Roman Boat Race**
Edward John Poynter

Oil on canvas

A DETAILED HISTORICAL setting, a basket of cherries, a palm fan and splendid jewellery all contribute to the exotic atmosphere of this painting, in which Poynter is trying to satisfy the public's thirst for images of ancient Rome. Poynter's artistic exploitation of antiquity began with a series of Egyptian paintings and he later moved on to Greek and Roman themes. Like Leighton and Alma-Tadema, Poynter provided classical images for the generation before the first cinema films brought scenes of Ancient Roman excess to life. As well as producing a considerable volume of work, Poynter dedicated a great deal of his time to teaching and administrating, first at the Slade School then at the Royal Academy, where he became President .

▷ **Pygmalion and the Image series** 1868-70
Edward Burne-Jones (1833-96)

Oil on canvas

EDWARD BURNE-JONES'S *Pygmalion and the Image* series of paintings is an interesting record of the Victorian middle-class attitude to love and sex. In the Ancient Greek legend of Pygmalion, the sculptor, who actually dislikes women, creates a statue of Venus with which he falls in love. Divine intervention brings the statue to life and makes him change his mind. In Burne-Jones's version the sculptor first dreams of his ideal woman – *The Heart Desires* – then, having created her, he does not dare to defile such beauty by touching it – *The Hand Refrains* (see page 58). Divine intervention in the form of an angel brings the statue to life, in a painting called *The Godhead Fires,* not included here. Having been given a flesh-and-blood ideal woman, the sculptor falls on his knees in adoration in the final painting in the series, *The Soul Attains* (see page 59). The sequence of paintings is in keeping with the Victorian ideal of the woman as wife and mother, placed by man on a pedestal to be worshipped: a very different being from the soiled dove who exists for his pleasure.

◁ **Pygmalion and the Image:
The Hand Refrains**

▷ **Pygmalion and the Image:
The Soul Attains**

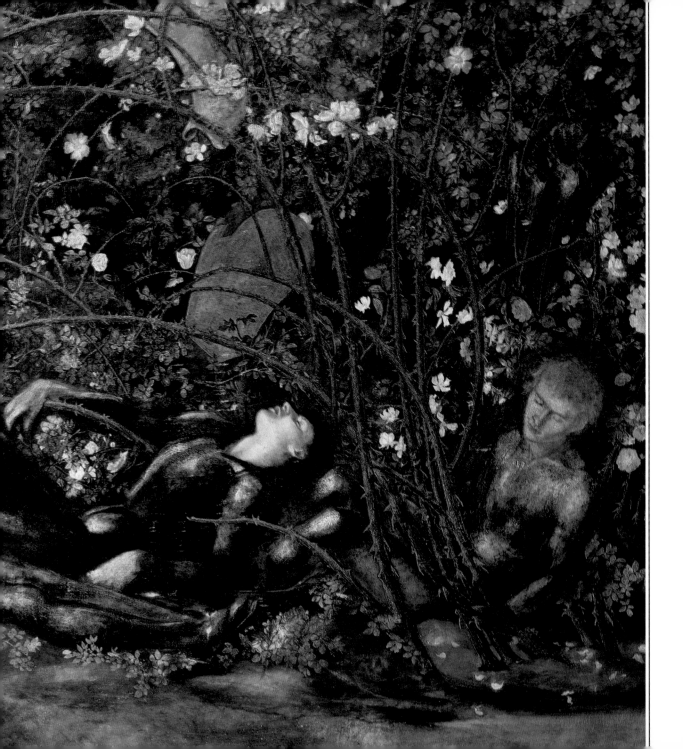

The Knights and the Briar Rose 1869
Edward Burne-Jones

Oil on canvas

◁ *Previous pages 60-61*

THIS PAINTING is part of a series with the mediaeval atmosphere that Burne-Jones loved. The theme is similar to that of the Sleeping Beauty: a fair princess in a wood and a bold knight to wake her from her sleep. The original fairy tale by Charles Perrault and Tennyson's poem 'The Day Dream' were the inspiration for Burne-Jones's painting. Here, the knights are caught in the briars of the wood but the hero is finding his way through. Burne-Jones has made a precise and delicate study of the briar rose but has not been quite so successful with the knights. The public, brought up on an idealized version of mediaeval times through Sir Walter Scott's novels, received this offering with acclamation.

▷ **The March Marigold**
c 1870
Edward Burne-Jones

Oil on canvas

BURNE-JONES met William Morris at Exeter College, Oxford, and the two became lifelong friends, sharing an enthusiaism for the work of the original Pre-Raphaelite painters. Burne-Jones had intended entering the Church but, with Morris, decided to devote his life to art instead. Despite having no formal training, though he received a few lessons from Rossetti, Burne-Jones became a prolific painter fired by Pre-Raphaelite ideas. In 1861 he went to Italy with Madox Brown and Rossetti and on his return helped to found Morris's design company, for which he supplied drawings for stained glass, tiles, tapestries and other items. The first Italian visit was followed by another, this time with Ruskin who persuaded him to make copies of Venetian paintings. This gave Burne-Jones a new technical mastery and brought him fame and a knighthood as the leader of a new era of painting.

◁ **King Cophetua and the Beggar Maid** 1884
Edward Burne-Jones

Oil on canvas

BURNE-JONES made many sketches for this painting whose mediaeval subject had a special appeal for him. The story is of a king who falls in love with a humble beggar maid whose beauty and purity (Tennyson described her as 'So sweet a face, such angel grace') are worth more than his kingdom. This is a typical Victorian morality story, the moral being that a good woman is worth more than earthly riches. One cannot help wondering how much the artist believed these sentiments, which seem to modern thinking a sop to the captive women in Victorian housholds. There is no uncertainty, however, about the quality of Burne-Jones's craftsmanship in this carefully composed painting, the designed space of which suggests an abstract composition.

▷ **The Baleful Head** 1886-87
Edward Burne-Jones

Oil on canvas

THE MEDUSA, one of the
Gorgons, had her hair turned
into writhing snakes by the
goddess Minerva for daring to
rival the goddess's beauty. No
one dared to look the Medusa
in the eye, for if they did they
were turned to stone. Perseus,
the Greek hero given the task
of cutting off the Medusa's
head, did so by looking at her
in the mirror of his polished
shield. In Burne-Jones's
depiction of this scene,
the displaying of the Medusa's
head becomes something like a
quiet moment at a garden
party when someone is
showing off travel souvenirs.
Thus a macabre tale is told in
a manner that does not offend
Victorian susceptibilities.
Paintings such as these also
had a vogue in Europe,
especially Germany, in the
latter part of the 19th century.

▷ **Proclaiming Claudius Emperor** 1867
Lawrence Alma-Tadema (1836-1912)

Oil on canvas

ALMA-TADEMA knew what the public wanted and he provided it with impeccable style. He also knew how to present history in a dramatic way and with popular appeal, as in this painting of Claudius being told by legionnaires that he is to be the next Emperor of Rome. Since he was expecting to be arrested, Claudius was surprised and so overcome that he fell on his knees before the soldiers. Alma-Tadema has painted the scene with meticulous attention to detail, setting it in one of the palace corridors where Claudius was hiding and showing the legionnaires, whom he depicts as ordinary young men, cheering their choice of Emperor to replace the tyrant Caligula.

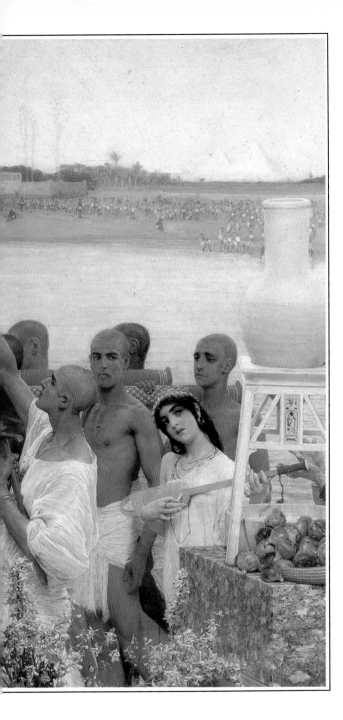

◁ **The Finding of Moses** 1902
Lawrence Alma-Tadema

Oil on canvas

THIS SCENE on the Nile, in
which an Egyptian princess,
the pharaoh's daughter,
receives Moses, who has just
been rescued from the river, is
worthy of a scene in a film by
Cecil B. De Mille. In fact,
Alma-Tadema and De Mille
were both fulfilling a similar
purpose, popularizng history.
Alma-Tadema may not have
been acceptable to the
partisans of the new aesthetic
movement in art but he was an
expert at illustrating great
moments in history. In making
studies for his compositions
Alma-Tadema made good use
of the new medium of
photography, which many
artists and art lovers despised.
He was an enthusiastic
photographer and left some
150 albums of his
photography, now kept at
Birmingham University.

▷ **A Coign of Vantage** 1895
Lawrence Alma-Tadema

Oil on canvas

LAWRENCE ALMA-TADEMA was a
Dutchman who became a
naturalized Englishman. He
began his painting life with
Baron Wappers, who had also
taught Ford Madox Brown.
Like Leighton, Alma-Tadema
painted the classical scenes
that had become popular
among the English middle
classes, who liked to see
themselves as latterday
Romans. Unlike Leighton,
who liked the mythological
past, Alma-Tadema painted the
daily life of Imperial Rome. In
this painting he shows three
Roman women looking out
from a high vantage point at
the arrival of the Roman fleet.
The superb technique of the
painter creates a sense of space
and distance and the
atmosphere of a sunny land.

△ **Pegwell Bay-A recollection of October 5, 1858**   William Dyce (1806-64)

Oil on canvas

DYCE CAME UNDER the influence of the German Nazarene painters during a visit to Rome in about 1825 and this led him naturally to an admiration for the Pre-Raphaelite painters, who had also been influenced by the German quasi-religious group. Dyce's scientific and intellectual pursuits did not allow him to devote himself exclusively to painting but he was superintendent of the School of Design in London in 1837 and won a competition for a decoration of the Houses of Parliament. *Pegwell Bay* is a well-observed landscape, probably helped by use of photography, and shows Dyce as an artist of considerable talent painting a sea coast that was soon to become a popular holiday destination.

△ **The Death of Chatterton** 1856   Henry Wallis (1830-1916)

Oil on canvas

WALLIS STUDIED at the Royal Academy schools and also at Gleyre's studio and the Beaux Arts in Paris between 1840-50. He was a prolific painter and in later years painted in Italy, Sicily and Egypt, but he made little impact in Britain. This picture of the death of the 17-year-old poet Thomas Chatterton, who committed suicide by taking arsenic, became his most famous work: it appealed to the sentimental Victorian weakness for stories of blighted hopes. Chatterton was a brilliant young poet, influencing Keats and Wordsworth, who called him 'the Marvellous Boy'. The model for the dead poet was George Meredith, whose wife later eloped with Wallis. The painting, executed in true Pre-Raphaelite style and with a great intensity of artistic feeling, was universally praised when it was exhibited at the Royal Academy and ended as the property of Augustus Egg who paid £200 for it. He had an engraving made of it, which soon became a popular ikon with a larger public.

◁ **April Love** 1855
Arthur Hughes (1832-1915)

Oil on canvas

HUGHES STUDIED under Alfred Stevens at Somerset House before going to the Royal Academy Schools. He became interested in the ideas and aims of the Pre-Raphaelites when he met Hunt, Rossetti and Brown in 1850 and Millais two years later. Soon after, he began to paint pictures symbolizing aspects of love. *April Love,* exhibited at the Royal Academy in 1856, was, as the title suggests, about young love and purity. When he first exhibited it, Hughes accompanied it with a quotation from a song in Tennyson's 'The Miller's Daughter':

'Love is hurt with har and fret.
Love is made a vague regret.
Eyes with idle tears are wet . . .'

He used several young women as models, but his favourite was Tryphena Foord whom he married. The model for the lover in the background was Hughes's friend Alexander Munro in whose Pimlico studio Hughes completed the painting he had begun at Maidstone.

△ **Pomegranates** 1866 Albert Moore (1841-93)

Oil on canvas

THOUGH NOT A MEMBER of the Pre-Raphaelite Brotherhood, Moore had many characteristics in common with the group. He was a most meticulous painter, making endless studies of his subjects, including nude studies for figures that he would later paint clothed. Like others of his period, he was influenced by Japanese art, the influence showing in his broad and simple compositions with a tendency to flatten forms. A talent for painting ran in his family; his father was a portraitist and his brother Henry a marine painter. A shy, reserved man, Moore did not become part of the Royal Academy establishment, though he exhibited at Academy shows. Moore did not usually bother to give special titles to his paintings for he considered them to be self-explanatory works of art.

▷ **The Visit of a Sick Child to the Temple of Aesculapius** (1877) John William Waterhouse (1847-1917)

Oil on canvas

WATERHOUSE was a late-Victorian painter much influenced by Burne-Jones and his Pre-Raphaelite manner. Born in Rome, he studied art there before joining the Royal Academy Schools in London in 1870. For a time he specialized in Roman subjects rather in the style of Alma-Tadema; later, his painting became looser, influenced perhaps by Impressionism and also by the aesthetic movement. This painting of a child visiting the temple of Aesculapius, the Greek god of healing, is painted in his classical style with every detail carefully observed in the interests of authenticity. Waterhouse's aim in painting was to 'reconcile Imagination and Realism'. He became R A. in 1895, a year after what is probably his most famous painting, *The Lady of Shalott,* was exhibited.

△ **Dolce Far Niente**   John William Godward (1861-1922)

Oil on canvas

'DOLCE FAR NIENTE' – 'Sweet idleness' – was a concept which appealed to many well-off Victorians with their supreme self-confidence and their delusions about having earned their reward by dint of hard work. Godward, like other late-Victorian artists, painted for the new rich, wealthy on the spoils of the Industrial Revolution and Britain's imperial strength, who expected a painter to turn out a picture with an opulent finish and who liked hedonistic themes. This lady lying on her rugs swathed in soft Grecian garments and with an opulent peacock fan tossed carelessly aside, is the epitome of the female as a rich man's ornament; evidence of his success in life.

▷ **The Lovers**
Simeon Solomon (1840-1905)

Oil on canvas

SIMEON SOLOMON, an orthodox
Jew, was an admirer of
Rossetti's late aesthetic period,
when the significance of
paintings was seen to lie in
their aesthetic values and had
a mixed sensual and spiritual
quality. Solomon's early
paintings often had subjects
taken from the Old Testament,
but after a visit to Italy in
1866-69, he was won over to a
more secular approach. He
himself was to convert to
Roman Catholicism. This
painting of two female lovers is
ambiguous in its meaning,
though it may have a biblical
connotation. Solomon's
paintings became increasingly
tainted with a maudlin
sentimentality and a distinctly
epicene tone. He gave way to
drink and dissipation which
destroyed first his talents and
eventually the man himself.

△ **Love the Conqueror** 1899   John Byam Liston Shaw (1872-1919)

Oil on canvas

THIS PAINTING brought into the open changing opinions about art current in England at the turn of the century. It was criticised for its Pre-Raphaelite inclination towards literature, which the *Daily Telegraph* newspaper's critic summed up by writing 'There is much that is trivial in presentment as in symbolism'. The *New York Times* critic, on the other hand hailed it as a painting with 'great originality of conception'. Shaw, who was an admirer of the work of Ford Madox Brown, did not disguise the symbolism of the picture, which shows a city capitulating to love, personified by youth and beauty, and famous lovers from world history following a captive female. Shaw painted a companion piece, a pageant of art and drama, which is hung in the London Coliseum, present home of the English National Opera.

ACKNOWLEDGEMENTS

The Publisher would like to thank the following for their kind permission to reproduce the paintings in this book:

Bridgeman Art Library, London/Birmingham City Museums and Art Gallery 14, 18, 41; /**Bradford Art Galleries and Museums** 33; /**Christie's, London** 29, 32, 42; /**Forbes Magazine Collection, London** 20-21, 46-47, 66-67; /**Joseph Setton Collection, Paris** 58,59; /**Guildhall Art Gallery, Corporation of London** 50-51, 74; /**Lady Lever Art Gallery, Port Sunlight** 24-25; /**The Maas Gallery, London** 48-49, 54, 60-61, 77; /**Manchester City Art Galleries** 8, 9, 15, 19, 34, 37, 39, 40; /**Piccadilly Gallery, London** 63; /**Private Collection** 44-45, 68-69, 70; /**Staatsgalerie, Stuttgart** 65; /**Tate Gallery, London** 10, 16-17, 26-27, 28, 30, 43, 52, 64, 72, 73; /**Towneley Hall Art Gallery and Museum, Burnley** 53; /**The Fine Art Society** 75,78; /**Victoria and Albert Museum** 35.